STAY WITH ME
poems from a year of beauty and ashes
Complete Second Edition

Amy Lutes

STAY WITH ME: poems from a year of beauty and ashes.
First edition, ©2020 Amy Lutes.
Complete second edition, ©2021 Amy Lutes.

ISBN: 979-8721535208

All rights reserved. No part of this book may be reproduced, or stored in a retrieval system, or transmitted in any form or by any means, electronic, mechanical, photocopying, recording, or otherwise, without express written permission of the publisher.

Cover designed using Canva.
Cover photo by Matteo Viviani from Getty Images.
Line drawings on cover and title page by joannewhyte.

foreword.

Twenty-twenty was a weird year. I didn't know it would be going into it, and on January 1st, I felt a burst of creative energy. I began the year throwing myself into digital found poetry.

By mid-March, we all began to realize that the year might be veering off the tracks a bit, but we had no idea just how much. I wanted to keep the poetry going, to bring a light into a dark space, but collective trauma slowed me down.

I didn't end up writing nearly as much as I'd wanted to, because, again, 2020 was weird. I wrote a total of 23 poems, and I was compelled to publish those in the first eBook edition of this book on December 31st. But I wanted to continue writing through mid-March, when things started getting real for me personally here in Nashville, TN.

These 52 poems you hold highlight joy and sadness, pain and hope. My wish is that somewhere in these tiny little snapshots, you find yourself. Or a piece of yourself you thought you lost a long time ago. Or something that will help you get through these strange times.

Whatever the case, I hope your 2021 and beyond turn out to be more balanced, and that you may find more beauty than ashes as you continue on your journey.

Always,

for everyone, everywhere

Table of Contents

remember.	1
linger.	2
uncharted magic.	3
sky full of hope.	4
blaze bright O sun.	5
trusted friend.	6
stagger.	7
moon.	8
grey wonder.	9
breathtaking radiance.	10
immaculate serene.	11
surreal reality.	12
tender balance.	13
come O muse.	14
in the Great Light.	15
hesitant hope.	16
dawning shimmer of hope.	17

are we.	18
wolf.	19
she is vibrant.	20
radiant promise.	21
stolen rose.	22
stay with me.	23
broken candlelight.	24
some whisper of home.	25
word transform me.	26
best thing.	27
liminal mystery.	28
hope is.	29
without escape.	30
lost in secret sorrow.	31
i see by blooming.	32
in an instant.	33
into existence.	34
light as breath.	35
uncertainty.	36

only pretending.	37
dead standstill rush.	38
armored heart.	39
wondering when.	40
strange new shores.	41
upside down.	42
hear me.	43
bitter swill.	44
somehow still bright.	45
here now.	46
the long road.	47
song of rebirth.	48
folds and fragments.	49
sink into you.	50
ever descending.	51
what to make of it.	52

Amy Lutes

remember.

remember
we seek our lost memories
    like an elusive jewel
        a secret enfolded
            into time
our silent wonder ascending
    uncertain
        unfulfilled
like breath into the
    quiet winter air

STAY WITH ME

linger.

we approach time dreaming,
    walking toward
        an empty eternity
on a dark silver sorrow.

Linger with me awhile
and if they try
    to break you,
        never
    surrender your magic.

Amy Lutes

uncharted magic.

a silver thread
      entwined us

    elusive
      sacred
        uncharted
      magic

between you and me

STAY WITH ME

sky full of hope.

sing the sky full of hope
           its fragrance
                descending
                      soft
like a
    whispered promise

or the last glow of
            light
          in the dark

Amy Lutes

blaze bright O sun.

   rising
eyes as fresh
  as a new day

blaze bright O sun
  encompass my shadows
    in your certain light

STAY WITH ME

trusted friend.

though i waver sometimes
    a fearful uncertain
            tremble
    you
    keep calling me

    trusted friend

stagger.

        stagger
a lost or withering
      sense of time
a thread
  a melody
    a canvas
      questioning the night

without you i am
  a rose in the rain
  a raven with a
      broken wing
  chilled and wanting

moon.

she the dream
    the shadow shining
a question lost
    in quiet wondering
heavenly muse
    a shrouded hunger
bright sacred flight
    awake without her

Amy Lutes

grey wonder.

autumn surrendered
　its chilled hesitation
　like gilded sadness
　passing through the sky

turning into an echo of
　　　　grey
　　　　　　wonder

STAY WITH ME

breathtaking radiance.

like a sea of stars or
glittering fields of galactic dust
    you are called into
        breathtaking radiance

do not obscure or
hide your light
with fear

    but seek out mystery
        and
    glow in the dark

Amy Lutes

immaculate serene.

sense the immaculate serene
   rolling in like the tide
watch as it breaks
     over the empty world

leaving a wake of
     beauty and wonder
 a soft mist rising
     toward the light

surreal reality.

        surreal
      reality
tries to shut us
    all into loneliness

our aching desire
      for gathering
will not save the world
   but it just might
     heal
       it

Amy Lutes

tender balance.

        contemplate
vision is found in
    the vibrant gold light
      of the sun
the hunger of a kiss
      that stops your breath
the patient stretching
     of roots and branches
as the mystery unfolds
   trust its tender
         balance

come O muse.

     come O muse
you wandering wonderer
of endless gilded realities

awake the brilliant fire
   within the words
      of this dreamer
that the blessed illusion
        might soar
    into waiting hearts

Amy Lutes

in the Great Light.

in the Great Light
there is no shadow
there is only
        light
    and other light
different colors
      different brightnesses
   but all still
light

hesitant hope.

imperfect
    I am aching
a rainbow of
    unfortunate dust
  falling soft onto
these burning fields
  of my
    hesitant hope

Amy Lutes

dawning shimmer of hope.

fiercely breathtaking
    I rise anew
        each morning
my value lies not
    in how strong I am
but in how I might
        lift you
    to see the
        dawning shimmer
          of hope

are we.

alone in the dark
between memories
I lie awake wondering
    am I
        are you
            are we
            lost somehow
                falling
            changing
        breaking trust
            are we

wolf.

    I realize the wolf
                is me
one with the beast
        I run with the beast
I explore beyond fear
      loyal to my instincts
                   alone

she is vibrant.

   she is vibrant
      her mind a blaze of
           sense and
         sensuous strength
     but all you do is
     silence her
       diminish her
         obscure her
    in the smoke of
    your uninvited
    guilt and shame

Amy Lutes

radiant promise.

within
the long silent
    sacred deep

seek
the radiant promise

it is
nearer than you think
waiting

    seeking
            you

stolen rose.

      stolen rose
    I was ten
I heard her scream and
    your struggle to control her
I think
    I hope
she got away and never looked
                             back
    for a long time after
    there was a hole
        in the hedgerow

    I never forgot

Amy Lutes

stay with me.

far flung stars
    veil an uncharted sea of glass
    lost shards of time and beauty
        soaring through radiant emptiness

all seems calm and quiet
      but stay with me
    for I am caught in the net
    of the rhythmic
          watery crash
        between sinking and rising

STAY WITH ME

broken candlelight.

a sudden withering
      a dark distortion
   befalls her

         a match flickers

broken candlelight
     dancing her
  into the shining light
     of day

Amy Lutes

some whisper of home.

    illusion
echoing through me
    surreal
the silent hunger
    aching

between the absurd or nothing
    give me some whisper
        of home

STAY WITH ME

word transform me.

strange magic
    your vision pulls me in
        wraps me into a soft cocoon
              of you
    warm
    protected
    safe
amid a dark-bright net of stars
        in our mind
             we coalesce

word
    transform me.

best thing.

    together
they reach toward a certain
    best thing
  suddenly
a shining thread in the tapestry
leads them far into a different
    best thing
  each without the other

liminal mystery.

liminal
mystery
the shore
is both
sand and sea
together
crashing
raging
against
each other
twisting
swirling
through
each other
constant
surrendering
sinking
into
belonging

Amy Lutes

hope is.

i feel a song rise
 with my desperate breath
  and pierce the
   chill watery evening

hope is
 a long lonely song
we somehow keep singing
 until the storm surrenders

STAY WITH ME

without escape.

no goodbye
         stay

    your
        whisper falters
           into the shadow
           into the silent heaviness
        of this mist
             engulfing us
             without escape

Amy Lutes

lost in secret sorrow.

when you find yourself
        lost in secret sorrow
            by the dazzling sea
      cast dark memories
     into the chill shadowy deep
but promise you will keep
        all the radiant beauty
            that belongs to you

i see by blooming.

shine on me softly
when your immaculate light
    is too much

i still need
    conversation and dreams

        but

i see by blooming
        not burning

Amy Lutes

in an instant.

she approaches the edge
    yearning for escape
        dark dreamer
           seemingly lost
but this is not
      a leap of fear
        but of faith

    in an instant
    soft wings open

  falling is rising
    dark is bright
lost is found

into existence.

```
dance
      yourself
              into
                    existence
like fire or the wild wind

perfection is found when
            you embrace you
                    knowing you are

wonderfully different
without jealousy
```

Amy Lutes

light as breath.

you hold within you
    light
        as breath
catch and release
        inhale and exhale
  true north star
  in your very soul
      like a
      secret
      radiant
      compass

uncertainty.

can we
embrace the aching breath
without our arms wavering
realizing the future
is hidden

this is a newfound kind of
balance for us
to be certain
of our
uncertainty

Amy Lutes

only pretending.

a step
        closer to our future
lovesick arms crave touch
but collapse around
        only air

only pretending
        desperate

we are nothing without each other

STAY WITH ME

dead standstill rush.

time is blooming blind
    flying slowly
        dead standstill rush

its touch
    might leave us
           distorted
but we are not as
        broken
as we like to think

Amy Lutes

armored heart.

armored heart
        protected body
memory calling into question
        these lost whispers
            of imperfect desire

hope threading its needle
        to close up the dark
    with patterns of color
        and light

STAY WITH ME

wondering when.

the closer the end seems
    the further it gets
        the longer it takes to
      reach it

we are all just
        wondering when

hope can be
  so seductive
  so surreal
    so endless

Amy Lutes

strange new shores.

   fresh life breaks through these shadows
like a renegade star at midnight
   illuminating the questions that
      burn for answers

follow the siren of wonder
   far into the depths
to wake on
   strange new shores

upside down.

upside
>you awaken
>stronger than before
>a soft but vibrant flame
>shining through the
>stained glass shards
>of your
>heart

>>down
>the questions
>the emptiness the
>struggle to believe that
>>you are still
>>worthy of
>>love

Amy Lutes

hear me.

fragments ascend
    away into the air
    like shattered pieces
    of emotions

        tears

we may sometimes
    falter or
    break
when your distorted need
    for power
    tries to silence us

hear me

we will blaze anyway

bitter swill.

poisoned reality
meaningless pretending

time itself can tremble and quake
and yet nothing changes

the deep yearning
    is met with laughter

the simple hope
    with crushing loss

the unending dreaming
    with the bitter swill of
    illusion and existence

Amy Lutes

somehow still bright.

the tender softness crashing into you
the uninvited collapse
the invisible wall

the waiting

the fervent whisper
the inexplicable laughter
the unfulfilled hope that is
         somehow still bright

it is surreal but true

it's a wonderful existence

STAY WITH ME

here now.

tend each tear
belong to one another

wander the world curious and kind
    between sorrow and wonder
        from sleeping to waking
            through shadow and light

seek vibrant vision
            here
                now
in a sea of unknown futures

Amy Lutes

the long road.

tonight
the dazzling moon
crowns the kind of
      clear silent sky
you can wish on

remember love

we are here together
for the long road

song of rebirth.

it's hard to sing
  when you are in
    dark uncharted waters
     many miles from
      where you began
       the dark lonely sky
        going on forever

        it's okay for you
        to be afraid

there is no song of rebirth
  without a womb experience

Amy Lutes

folds and fragments.

we fall and rise
   imperfect but stunning

our thread weaves to and fro
      into folds and fragments
      drawing together both
         bright colors and dark

we go where the weaver guides us
      drawing a broken world
         together into beauty

sink into you.

hold me
my heart is breaking
the world is changing
the future is missing so many

> let me sink into you
> fold into your soul
> so my whole being
> resonates with the song
> of you

Amy Lutes

ever descending.

the sun
        ever descending
opens to our existence
        the door to time and space

we keep thinking it is empty
        but we have already
                stepped through it
      and yet
            we still question
            our own intuition

STAY WITH ME

what to make of it.

the world is breaking
    fraying at the seams
we each hold a piece
and wonder
    what to make of it

even in a year like this
    we can hold
    beauty
    in our hands
    breath
    in our lungs
    hope
    in our hearts

what will we make of it
        of this world
        of this year
        of this life

About the Author:

Amy Lutes is a poet, author, artist, and nature lover hailing from Middle Tennessee, where she lives with her husband and two children. She has big dreams of using words and story in a way that can bring healing to people, especially to women who have experienced trauma.

Amy holds a BA in English Language & Literature and a graduate certificate in Theopoetics, and is currently working toward ordination in the Church of the Nazarene. Her current works-in-progress include a mixed-media and found poetry series that deconstructs purity culture, rewriting damaging messages into poems of hope and healing; and a YA dystopian series.

You can find Amy at:

amylutes.com
@amyluteswriter on Facebook, Instagram, and Twitter

Also by Amy Lutes:

Baptism: On Sinking and Rising

Made in the USA
Monee, IL
06 April 2021